J. S. Potter

The Past, Present and Future of Boston

Speech of Hon. J.S. Potter on the Subject of uniting certain Cities and

Towns with the City of Boston

J. S. Potter

The Past, Present and Future of Boston
Speech of Hon. J.S. Potter on the Subject of uniting certain Cities and Towns with the City of Boston

ISBN/EAN: 9783337154103

Printed in Europe, USA, Canada, Australia, Japan

Cover: Foto ©ninafisch / pixelio.de

More available books at **www.hansebooks.com**

The Past, Present and Future of Boston.

SPEECH

OF

Hon. J. S. POTTER,

OF ARLINGTON,

ON THE SUBJECT OF

UNITING CERTAIN CITIES AND TOWNS WITH THE CITY OF BOSTON:

DELIVERED IN THE

Massachusetts Senate, Thursday, April 24, 1873.

PRINTED BY ORDER OF THE SENATE.

BOSTON:
WRIGHT & POTTER, STATE PRINTERS,
19 PROVINCE STREET.
1873.

PROCEEDINGS IN THE SENATE.

Hon. CARROLL D. WRIGHT, of Middlesex, introduced the following Order which was adopted and then referred to the Committee on Printing.

COMMONWEALTH OF MASSACHUSETTS.

IN SENATE, April 29, 1873.

Ordered, That two thousand copies of the speech delivered in the Senate by Hon. Mr. Potter, on the subject of the annexation of certain towns and cities to the city of Boston be printed for the use of the legislature.

S. N. GIFFORD, *Clerk*.

Subsequently the committee submitted the following Report. which was accepted. and the Order was then passed.

COMMONWEALTH OF MASSACHUSETTS.

IN SENATE, April 30, 1873.

The Committee on Printing, to whom was referred the Order that two thousand copies of the speech delivered by Hon. Mr. Potter, on the subject of the annexation of certain cities and towns to the city of Boston be printed for the use of the Legislature, report that the Order ought to pass.   Per order,

J. K. BANISTER.

SENATE, April 30, 1873.

Accepted.

S. N. GIFFORD, *Clerk*.

ACTION OF THE COMMITTEE.

On January 4th, Mr. Potter, on leave, introduced an Act entitled " An Act to enlarge the territory of, and unite certain towns and cities with, the city of Boston." The towns and cities proposed for union under one municipality, were as follows :—

The city of Chelsea and the towns of Winthrop and Revere. in the county of Suffolk ; the cities of Charlestown, Somerville and Cambridge. and the towns of Malden. Everett. Medford, Arlington. Belmont and Watertown and Brighton, in the county of Middlesex ; and the towns of West Roxbury and Brookline. in the county of Norfolk.

The Bill was referred to the Committee on Towns, consisting of Hon. Martin Griffin, of Suffolk. Hon. Newton Morse. of Middlesex, of the Senate. and Benj. F. Hayes, of Medford, John Nowell. of Boston, G. P. Kendrick, of Worcester, N. D. Ladd. of Sturbridge, and George Purington, Jr., of Mattapoisett, of the House.

On the 16th of April the committee submitted the following Report and accompanying Resolve.

COMMONWEALTH OF MASSACHUSETTS.

IN SENATE, April 16, 1873.

The Committee on Towns, to whom was referred the Bill to enlarge the territory of, and unite certain towns and cities with the city of Boston, have considered the matter, and report the accompanying Resolve.

NEWTON MORSE.

COMMONWEALTH OF MASSACHUSETTS.

RESOLVE in relation to uniting certain Cities and Towns with the City of Boston.

Resolved, That the governor, with the advice and consent of the council, appoint a commission, consisting of three able and discreet persons, to report, after due investigation, upon the practicability and expediency of uniting with the city of Boston, under one municipal government, the following cities and towns:—The city of Chelsea and the towns of Winthrop and Revere, in the county of Suffolk; the cities of Charlestown, Somerville and Cambridge, and the towns of Malden, Everett, Medford, Arlington, Belmont and Watertown, in the county of Middlesex; * and what portion of the territory of such cities or towns, or any of them, in their judgment it would be expedient to so annex. Such investigation and report to include an examination of the feasibility and policy of such a union: the commercial, economical, industrial, sanitary and other considerations relating thereto; the mode of consummating the same, if deemed practicable and expedient; and whatever else may pertain to the municipal polity of a territory and people so connected and identified, as well with reference to their own good government and well-being as to the general welfare of the Commonwealth.

Said commission may employ all necessary assistance, and shall report the results of their investigation to the next legislature, embodying the same in a proper bill, if they shall deem legislation expedient, and shall be allowed for their compensation and expenses such sums as shall be approved by the governor and council, not to exceed five thousand dollars.

* The towns of Brookline, Brighton and West Roxbury were not embraced in this Resolve for the reason that Bills providing for their annexation to Boston were presented to the legislature before the Committee made their Report upon this subject.

SPEECH.

Mr. President:

There is no duty which I feel called upon to perform that is to me more unpleasant than that of occupying a moment of the time of the Senate in explaining measures which impress me as being of public interest. But the subject under consideration seems to me of such transcendant importance in its bearings upon the interests of the people of Boston and vicinity—and of the entire Commonwealth as well —that I trust I may be excused for asking the ear, and perhaps the exercise of the patience, of the Senate, while I endeavor to present some facts and general considerations connected with the past, present and future of Boston, that may be of possible value to those who feel an interest in the growth and prosperity, as well as in the health and happiness of the people of the metropolis of Massachusetts.

The Resolve reported by the committee provides for the appointment of a commission of three able and discreet men, vested with all the power neces-

2

sary to enable them to thoroughly investigate the
subject of uniting the city of Boston and the fifteen cities and towns enumerated in the bill which
I laid before the Senate at the opening of the present session; and if the commission shall deem expedient, they are authorized to prepare a wiser and
more carefully considered measure for the consum-
mation of such union. I would not have so great
a reform hurried to completion with such rapidity
that all necessary knowledge relating to it cannot
be obtained, because when it is done, it should be
well and properly done. I therefore cheerfully
accept the conclusions of the committee as being
wise and prudent, and will proceed to present some
reasons why the Resolve should pass, and why such
union appears to me not only desirable, but an
indispensable necessity.

Sir, knowledge is the creation of industry :—that
is, it springs from an active body and an active
mind. If that activity is compulsory, or the result
of necessity, then knowledge is acquired slowly, or
rather worked out through unseen difficulties by
the hard and tedious process of unaided toil. Such
is the experience, and such the school, of the pio-
neer. But the sagacious and observing student
who follows, will pursue the shorter and more direct path which is always before him. He will
"reap where others have sown." He will study
the lessons of the past, and profit by the revelations
of departed ages. He will not permit the dust and

cobwebs of time to conceal the obstacles which his
fathers encountered or the errors which they com-
mitted, but will behold the future by the light of
their experience, and thus be able more wisely to
measure its demands upon the present. He will
look upon existence as a progressive fact, no more
designed to halt upon the accomplishments of the
hour, than was the revolving globe upon which we
live designed to stand still. He will regard ideas
as creations which are never to mature, and look
upon them as the school-boy looks upon the ball
which he begins rolling in the adhesive snow—as
conceptions which are to grow with every revolu-
tion they make through the force of mental and
physical action. Ideas which spring from intelligent reflection are ever in conflict with those that
are born of impulse; and the government or the
man that moves in obedience to impulse, and acts
only with reference to the exigencies of the hour,
is simply placing obstructions in the path of progress, which will surely retard, though never prevent, the march of the ever-coming future from
sweeping such obstructions away; thus making re-
construction and its attendant consequences of delay
and heavy taxation a necessity and a burden upon
the advance of civilization.

THE EARLY DAYS OF BOSTON AND THE ERRORS OF
ITS FOUNDERS.

Two hundred and fifty years ago an intelligent
Englishman landed upon the shores of Massachusetts Bay. His sagacity and good judgment induced him to select for his home a locality among
the blueberry bushes and other shrubbery that
covered the peninsula at the junction of Charles
River and the waters of the harbor. Here, prefer-
ring seclusion to society, that "memorable man,"
William Blackstone, built a cottage, in which he
was a solitary dweller for many years. In the
meantime a flourishing settlement under Governor
Winthrop had been established opposite to his
cottage on the other side of the river. In the year
1630 many of the inhabitants of this settlement,
which was called Charlestown, became sick and
discontented. While their troubles were most
pressing, some of their leading men rowed across
the river and sought the counsel of the kind-
hearted Blackstone. He recommended as a pana-
cea for their ills, even at that early day,—not exactly annexation, but the next thing to it,—that
they should move over to "his side of the river."
There was room enough to apply his remedy
then, but not now. They followed Blackstone's
advice, Governor Winthrop leading, his house
having been first carried over for his accommodation.

Thus began the settlement which they "agreed to call Boston." The city which has grown from this small beginning, has not yet honored in a becoming manner the name of William Blackstone, who discovered in the spot upon which it stands, with its surroundings, a locality which, as I hope to show, has no parallel in the advantages which it presents for the prosperous existence of one of the most healthful and beautiful cities on this continent, or in the world.

Here, at the base of the three promontories whose tops caught the refreshing breezes of land and sea, the followers of Blackstone and Winthrop moved forward with their incipient city. One would have thought that the startling events which were at that time happening in the compact cities which were being desolated with fires and plagues in the "Old World," with which they were so familiar, would have been efficient lessons to those who were laying the foundation of a new city, where land could be had for five shillings per acre. The handcart and an occasional passing team served the business demands of their day, and they constructed ways only wide enough for their accommodation. It is true they had come here to populate a new continent and inaugurate a work which would require ages to complete; yet the simple needs of the hour were their guide. They saw only that future which reached beyond this life to the shores of immor-

tality. Therefore, they worked without plans,
system or method. In laying out a city that was
to be "built with hands" they permitted their im-
pulses to seize upon the accidental cow path and
the milkmaid's walk, and these they followed
as leading suggestions. Thus, though pioneers of
advanced civilization in a "New World," they
started with the most absurd errors of the "Old
World" in the practical business of laying out a
city which would, according to every teaching of
history, at some future date, not remote, be occupied by millions of people. Indeed, they do not
appear to have measured at all the possible needs
of posterity. For light, circulation of air, health
and security from pestilence and conflagration were
not catalogued in their minds as matters to be considered in connection with the construction of a
city. The exigency of the hour seems to have
been their guide in practical affairs; and this
most pernicious and evil practice has adhered, like
a leech, to our state, city and town legislation
down to the present hour.

With an ever-growing intelligence, impelled by
the activity and industry which were characteristic
of the founders of Boston, what result could follow
such a policy? Why, then as now, every new
year developed new conditions and new demands,
for which the old one, for lack of ordinary fore-
thought, had not provided. Thus began the work
of undoing, to correct errors, of pulling down and

building up.—resulting in a wastefulness of time and means which has continued to the present time and is now in full operation. Mistakes even were corrected only with a view to meet the necessities of the time. The future seems never to have been provided for. And this state of things, which has been a perpetual drag upon the prosperity of the city, has been growing worse with the increase of population, until

THE ENORMOUS COST OF CORRECTING PAST ERRORS

has become at the present day a serious burden upon the inhabitants of Boston and its vicinity. The founders of the city, and those who succeeded them, shut out the light and air of heaven from its streets, which they huddled together in promiscuous confusion, in order that they might save a few feet of land which cost a farthing a foot. But the third generation following, with a view of providing for growing public necessities, has been obliged, not only to pull down and rebuild costly structures, but at the same time to pay from five to thirty thousand times that sum for the same land, now needed to double and treble the width of their original narrow and contracted thoroughfares. Now, sir, this same confused system of planning, and this same short-sighted policy of the past, is to-day practised in portions of the city of Boston, and in all the cities and towns within the territory which it is now proposed to unite with it. The con-

venience of the hour still appears to be the mis-
chievous sentiment ruling in the council chamber
and town meeting.

If Senators will consult the records at the City
Hall they will be astonished to learn that there are
instances where streets have been widened two,
three and even four times on the *same line* to
meet the growing demands for room, and each
time at a heavy cost to the tax-payer, when such
changes would not have been necessary if the
people and those in power had simply remembered,
as I now ask *you* to remember, that "the world
moves," and has a future to provide for which
should always commend itself to the consideration
of thoughtful law-makers everywhere.

Sir, if the present policy is to continue, no comprehensive public improvements will be possible,
for the reason that all the revenue, and much more
than is needed for such purposes, will continue to
be swallowed up in correcting the errors, which,
under it, seem ever to follow in the track of state
and municipal legislation.

As an illustration of the prodigal effects of this
"convenience-of-the-hour legislation," I will refer
to but one of many examples. Hanover Street,
which was one of the paths where the milkmaid
followed the tinkling bell of the "lowing herd," has
been widened in some places two or three times,
and yet another widening has just been completed,
at a cost to the tax-payers and abutters of nearly

$2,500,000 more. I will not attempt to predict the period when another slice from the costly structures that have been rebuilt upon this busy avenue may be necessary; but I will ask Senators to stand for a moment at any hour of the day, and view the active throng that already moves therein, when Boston has a population of only one-quarter of a million, and at the same time remember that the deep waters of her ample harbor bound this and other streets, now of less capacity, where the active commercial enterprise of the city must be forever carried on. For, while the city will rapidly expand, the harbor must ever remain substantially the same, till the pressure of a continent's exports necessitates the construction, in the rear of Charlestown, of vast docks like those of London. I will then ask you to pass over, in imagination, a period of fifty years, when the locks of the youngest Senators at this board will be whitened by time and when the population of Boston will be ten times as great as now, with her industries multiplied by a still larger figure; and then give your judgments as to the capacity of any or all of these avenues, as now constructed, to comfortably accommodate even a considerable fraction of the business that will then move to and from the teeming wharves and the railroad termini that must necessarily cluster about them.

It is now fifty years since the city government of Boston was established. Since that time about

three hundred of her streets, lanes, and courts have
been widened or altered to meet the demands of
growing business for more liberal accommodations,
—making an average of almost six streets a year
for the entire period. The total cost of these alterations, including interest, has been a sum fully
equal to the valuation of all the real property of the
entire city fifty years ago. The loss to the people
arising from their restricted conveniences for doing
business is another very important item which is
not embraced in this calculation.

During the *last six* years fifty-five streets have
been enlarged; and the expense of this work,
including the estimated cost for alterations on
others which it has been decided to extend and
widen, will amount to the startling sum of twenty-
one millions of dollars or more. A little intelligent
foresight in providing for the growth of the city
would have saved the people of to-day from
the burden of such a vast expenditure, which must
now be borne alike by Boston and surrounding
towns; for a resident of Malden, Cambridge, Brookline or Chelsea, who owns property and does business in Boston, simply has the privilege of paying
two taxes,—one, to defray the expense of the
municipality which governs him while he sleeps,
and another to the municipality which governs him
while pursuing his business.

Now, sir, this sum, virtually squandered by the
effects of the pinched and short-sighted legislation

of the past would, if judiciously expended, have laid
out and completed, within the same brief period,
six spacious avenues, each six miles long and one
hundred and forty feet wide, in different directions
straight through the entire territory which it is now
proposed to embrace within the limits of ONE city,
allowing $300,000 per mile for construction, shade
trees, and other ornamentations. In addition to
these improvements it would have purchased for
park purposes in different portions of this territory,
three thousand acres of land, at $1,500 per acre,
admirably adapted to such purposes. So that four
parks, each nearly as large as the famous Central
Park in New York City, and all much nearer the
centre of population, could have been provided for,
and there would still remain nearly $6,000,000 with
which to improve and beautify them. A sum, sir,
just about equal to the entire expenditures for improvements upon Central Park.

Vauban, when speaking of the great French
metropolis, as long ago as the time of Louis the
Fourteenth, said truly: "Paris is to France what
the head is to the human body; it is the true heart
of the kingdom." Believing that Boston does
now, and will continue to occupy a similar relation
to our old Commonwealth, and believing that
whatever promotes the welfare and prosperity of
the metropolis will be equally beneficial to the whole
State, I feel justified in asking Senators if it is not
time that some plan should be devised which will

check the prevailing short-sighted system of building up only to pull down again,—whether more
economical, because more comprehensive, legislation should not be initiated, which will not only
meet the exigencies of the hour, but which, observing the rule of the past, will intelligently measure
the self-evident demands of coming centuries?
The lessons of experience plainly teach us

HOW TO AVOID A REPETITION OF PAST ERRORS.

Ample territorial space for expansion is the
first necessity,—to provide for it while it is com-
paratively cheap is the first duty. The Resolve before the Senate is a step in this direction. It proposes an intelligent and careful investigation of
the proposition to enlarge the area of Boston by
uniting with it the territory encompassed by the
beautiful range of highlands that extend from
Dorchester—ward sixteen—in the form of a cres-
cent, nearly around to Chelsea, forming a perfect
natural boundary to the limits of the city.

The territory of Boston is now shapeless. The
State House and the bulk of the population are located in one corner of it. The extreme eastern and
southern limits extend in a direct line about seven
miles from the City Hall. If the area is extended
in other directions, as proposed in the Metropolitan
District Bill, which I had the honor to submit to
the Senate, the plan of which is fully delineated
upon the map now suspended in front of the presi-

dent's chair, the State House will occupy a central position; the population being about equally distributed in all directions, from that point to the boundary line.

The bounds of the old town of Boston extended, as now proposed, from Chelsea to Brookline, and included both. Chelsea was set off in 1738, and Brookline in 1705, after prolonged opposition, because of the inconvenience of having but one voting place in the town,—and the area of Boston was thus reduced to less than seven hundred acres. The rapid growth of the city within this circumscribed space soon obliged its business men to domicile in various directions outside of its limits. The boundaries of the city have, however, from time to time, been extended, though wholly in one direction,—which accounts for the ridiculous and laughable figure it presents upon the map,— until its dimensions have increased about fifteen times, covering at this date an area of more than ten thousand acres.

Now this bill simply proposes to extend the limits of Boston east, north and north-west, so as to make the distance of its boundary lines in those and all other directions almost exactly what it now is in the south-east and south-west, taking Beacon Hill as a central point from which to measure. The range of highlands which encircle this territory forms a basin within which are located Boston and the fifteen smaller municipalities which it is

proposed to unite with it. While this basin contains nearly the same number of square miles as
Philadelphia or the city of London, it is of vastly
better proportions, and is divided by three rivers,
—the Charles, Mystic, and Malden,—with a fourth,
the Neponset—on its southern boundary. The
city of Philadelphia covers an area twenty-three
miles long and five and a half miles wide, and portions of her park grounds are more than twenty
miles from the centre of population; while the
outer limits of the territory covered by the towns
and cities named in the Resolve can be reached
within seven miles in any direction from the State
House. There are, also, in different parts of it,
six picturesque and delightfully situated little
lakes, which will average in size more than one
hundred acres each, besides four or five smaller
sheets of water not less beautiful. These are all
fed and kept pure by springs and the numerous
streams that flow down the sides of the extensive
highlands that surround them.

Economy and good taste suggest that these
sheets of water should be embraced in parks. The
lakes in the great parks of other cities of the
world, are artificial, and have been constructed at
an immense cost. Those in Central Park, New
York, are located upon land once laid out into
streets and lots. Nature has here provided larger
and better ones—all easily accessible to the mass
of the population; and, inasmuch as the great

ponds belong to the Commonwealth, they could be
secured for public use *without cost*, and would
thus largely reduce the price per acre for park
reservations.

The chorography of the land is diversified, being
hills, plains and slopes, the lowest of these—except a small tract of salt-water marsh—lying considerably above tide-water, thus affording superior opportunities for economical and perfect
drainage,—a consideration of the very highest
importance to a locality that is to contain, as this
basin eventually will, millions of human beings,
whose health should be the first thought of government. There are, too, some spots yet remain-
ing where the natural forest growth has not been
disturbed, and which would be of priceless value
if they could be embraced in park reservations.

Here, then, are all the elements of comfort,
beauty, and health: the numerous slopes and
plains, with their background of mountains and
hills, and the gleam of fresh, sparkling, shining
water; and "water in the landscape," as has been
said, "is like eyes in the human countenance,
without which the countenance is lifeless." There
are elevations upon these beautiful highlands
from the top of which the visitor can look down
upon forty cities and towns, and upon all the islands
in our ample harbor, where myriad sails are waft-
ing the commerce of the nation in every direction,
presenting in the commingled works of God and

man, a scene of magnificent grandeur which is
not rivalled by any other spot on earth. If in
Europe, this locality would be renowned as the
resort of tourists and sight-seers from every land;
but there is not one in a thousand of the population of our own state that even knows of its existence; yet, sir, it is within thirty minutes' ride
from the steps in front of this chamber, and ought
long since to have been an attractive spot in one of
the parks of Boston.

The most distant part of this territory is only
about six miles from deep-sea water at the head of
one of the most commodious and safe harbors upon
the coast of the Atlantic Ocean, and is the nearest
convenient port in the United States to the markets
of Europe. Could the hand of nature have planned
a more inviting locality for a city of vast population and boundless prosperity?

To those who have studied the characteristics of
Boston and its environs, it has been a subject of
wonder that all this area has not long ere this been
embraced under one government, and subject to an
harmonious and general system of improvement,
directed by judicious and liberal municipal legislation. Who but those immediately familiar with the
fact, like yourselves, would believe that the most intelligent and industrious people in the world, would,
for more than two hundred years, have been content
with being huddled together upon a narrow peninsula, without taking the first step toward per-

fecting some comprehensive arrangement which
would secure, for the benefit of the population rapidly accumulating here, the remarkable advantages
which the locality presents for an economical development of all that is useful, beautiful, and healthful? Would you believe that a people willing to
hazard the perils of a voyage across the Atlantic
Ocean to see the gardens, parks, and boulevards of
Paris, have not yet, with all their wealth and enterprise, and vastly superior opportunities, planned a
single one for themselves, even where nature has
done more than half the work; nor constructed a
single spacious avenue, where there should have
been at least a dozen, extending out in to the country beyond the city limits?

In addition to the peculiar advantages of her
maritime location, Boston has nearly every other
desirable requisite to secure unlimited prosperity
for her people, except an abundance of territorial
area within her own control, which should extend,
not in one, but in every direction where her
growth will be most natural. Without this she
must ever remain, what in a business sense she now
is, simply the office, the salesroom, the storehouse,
the bank and mainly the distributing point of New
England. The element that builds up and sustains
the substantial growth of a great city is employment
for the masses of its population that will be certain
and remunerative, and it is only by being relieved

4

from her circumscribed limits upon a narrow peninsula that

BOSTON CAN BECOME A GREAT MANUFACTURING CENTRE.

To be something more than a counting-room, and to support in a thriving condition the population that is rapidly gathering around her, she must rely upon and encourage manufactures. And these, to be prosperous, should be subject to one government and have a uniform system of care, taxation, and protection. Cheap building sites for mechanics, and eligible localities for their industries, though a *sine qua non* to the thrift and attractions of a great city, cannot be obtained or afforded within the present limits of Boston. And, sir, since land is abundant and accessible, and methods for cheap and swift transit in cities are being rapidly developed, I hope we have arrived at that point of sanitary knowledge and civilization which will hereafter prevent the poorer classes from being crowded into alleys, lanes, and narrow streets, where disease will be generated and epidemics revel.* For the reason that their

* The following is the closing paragraph of an interesting paper, read at the Lowell Institute in 1870, by FRANCIS BACON:—

"These cities of the future, with sunlight and fresh air and pure water coming to every citizen; with no one standing in his neighbor's way; with no noisome or pernicious occupation suffered within their limits; with all rainfall and water-waste carried quickly away to the unharmed river, while all other refuse, at once more dangerous and valuable, goes with due dispatch to the hungry soil; with order and cleanliness and beauty in all the streets; with preventable diseases prevented, and with inevitable ones skilfully cared for; with the vigilant

families are generally more numerous, they need as much living room as those more favored with the means of obtaining it. And it is alike for their interests and the economy of the entire community that broad streets and open spaces should be provided, so that under suitable regulations they would be induced to locate their homes where light, sunshine, air, and the foliage of trees may ever exist to dispel miasms, and act as guardians of the public health. Such an arrangement would not only be more agreeable but much cheaper than providing poor-houses and hospitals, to be maintained at the public expense.

The prosperity and wealth of a state can be measured by the amount of its manufactures; and any legislation that will increase them is a benefaction to mankind. What has built up Philadelphia, with its monotonous surroundings, but its manu-

government that does not stand apart and look coldly at ruthless greed and needy ignorance, and utter only an indifferent 'caveat emptor,' but says to the butcher, 'This trichinous pork, this pathological beef, goes to the rendering-vat, and not into the mouths of my children'; and to the brewer, 'Burn this cocculus indicus and lobelia, and let me see no bitter but hops hereafter'; and to the apothecary, 'Successor of Herod, you shall not poison my infants at wholesale with your narcotic "soothing sirups"'; and to the water company, 'Your reservoir shows foulness this week to my microscope and my test-tube; let it continue at your peril.' These cities of the minimum death-rate, shall they not be our cities? Are these things of impracticable costliness, say you? Nothing is so cheap as health; it is the truest economy; it is cheaper than dirt. 'Dirt cheap'—what an abuse of language! Dirt means waste and disease, death, widowhood, orphanage, pauperism, high taxation, costly production. Nothing costs so much. Besides, the objection [to cost] even if it were not unfounded, is unworthy. 'All parsimony in war is murder,' is a judicious maxim of the Maréchal de Belleisle. Not less, I say, when we fight against an impersonal foe of mankind."

factories and the fostering care the city has bestowed
upon them? What has nearly doubled the prosperity and population of the great city of London in a
single decade, but the productions that come from
the busy hands of twelve hundred thousand artisans
and mechanics? And what has made Paris the
pride of France, and of the world, but the manufac-
tories within her limits, that furnish unceasing
employment to more than six hundred thousand
artisans?

Now, sir, I hazard nothing in saying that not
within the limits of either of these great cities, nor
in any city upon this continent, do manufacturing
advantages exist which will at all compare with
those embraced within the surroundings of Boston. Under the lead of science and inventive
skill, we are rapidly approaching, if we have not
already reached, the day when steam-power at
tide-water markets, convenient for export and
import traffic, will, for all kinds of manufacturing
purposes, be found more economical and profit-
able than inland water-power, for the reason that
the cost of railroad freights to and from the inland factories will be greater than the cost of all
the water-carried fuel which may be necessary to
generate the more certain and reliable power of
steam. For instance, why has the flourishing city
of Fall River advanced with such marvellous rapidity to the foremost place among the manufacturing
localities of New England? Her location upon

tide-water is the first reason, and the intelligent en-
couragement which has been bestowed upon her
manufacturing industries by the people through
her local government, and by using home capital
for the development of home interests, completes
the answer. Here, too, may be studied with profit
the influence of municipal power in shaping the
industrial destinies, and promoting the thrift of
masses of people.

The waters of the Delaware and Schuylkill flow
through Philadelphia, the Thames through London, and the Seine through Paris, while Boston,
under the proposed organization, would have a
tide-water front superior to either of them, upon
which cargoes and supplies from all parts of the
world could be carried almost to the factory doors
without transhipment. In addition to this advantage, there will flow through the northern sections
of the city the Mystic and Malden rivers, and
through the southern section the Neponset; while
the larger Charles, with its tidal forces, ever act-
ing as the purifier and sanitary agent of the great
city, and coursing like the life-giving aorta,—not
on the boundary, but as nature would have it,
through the *centre* of the city,—sweeping into the
sea all the sewage and putrescence which an improved system of drainage would pour into it. In-
terspersed between these rivers are the nine little
lakes and the numerous streams that feed them, so
that here the morning and evening bells, or the

shriller steam-whistle, would never want for power
to sound the presence of countless industries.

Hence, if the teachings of facts are to be our
guide, I say that the years are not remote when,
under a single system of government, and with
appropriate state and municipal legislation, the
Island Ward and the Peninsula or "North End"
of Boston and the banks of these rivers will be
dotted with magnificent factory structures; and
while the people who now throng the pinched
and crooked streets of the northern portions of
the city will be obliged to seek healthier homes in
broader streets beyond the present limits of Boston, new occupations for them will rise upon the
places they vacate.

But, it will be asked, how is the union of this
territory with Boston to influence the introduction
of new enterprises in arts and manufactures? One
answer, among many, is, that the advantages which
it presents for such purposes are not now known,
and cannot be known while they are screened within a labyrinth of independent municipalities, all
working at cross purposes, and each in its isolated
character too small and weak to have any local or
general celebrity that will bring it prominently
before the eyes of the public. They maintain independent boundaries, it is true, and yet are so
near to the city of Boston as to be almost entirely
eclipsed under her shadow, and, therefore, in their
present position, neither enjoy the benefits of their

own nor the individual characteristics of the greater city which they adjoin; and thus they are but obstacles to each other, preventing those improvements which would bring to light the peculiar advantages of each locality, and in that way be so largely beneficial to all by attracting trade and capital from beyond the borders of the state and from other countries.

The instincts as well as the intelligence of man invite him to go where the sources of attraction are, where evidences of enterprise and thrift exist, and where the senses are gratified by elements of beauty and comfort. The eye of the active, thinking, inventive portions of mankind throughout the civilized world, is ever searching for localities where capacity may reap its reward, where capital and genius have an open and inviting field, and where opportunity and advantages will give industry a fair chance for success. That field is here, and this most desirable class of people will occupy it, if the scattered strength of the sixteen municipalities which now divide its possession shall be united under one homogeneous, progressive, representative government. With the markets of Europe on one side and a teeming continent with its productions and demands upon the other, the hands of hundreds of thousands of artisans would never want for remunerative employment to make their homes happy and themselves contented.

A RAPID GROWTH OF CITIES IS ONE OF THE LAWS OF THE AGE,

and the tendency of the people of the Nineteenth
century to concentrate in populous localities has
become so marked that no intelligent observer will
ask for proof in confirmation of the fact. A wise
foresight will make provision for this characteristic of the times, while it can be easily and
economically done, and conduct it to grand and
useful results. The increase in the population of
cities in all civilized countries for the last two or
three decades has been from one hundred to one
thousand per cent. greater, in proportion, than in
the country districts. Glasgow is growing six
times as fast as all Scotland; the rate of increase
in London, as compared with the rural districts of
England, is still larger; while Paris absorbs half
the increase of all France. In Russia, when eman-
cipation gave freedom to the serfs to go where
they pleased, a law had to be enacted to gradually
compensate the nobles for losses which they would
sustain by the depopulation of certain parts of the
country, on account of the eagerness of the peas-
antry to move into cities and large towns. Compare the increase of the population in one of the
best farming counties of Massachusetts—Franklin,
for instance—with that of Boston and adjoining
towns. The average increase for five years in
Franklin County has been considerably less than

one per cent. annually, while in Boston and the towns proposed for union, the average annual increase has been nearly six per cent. or more than six times as great as in the farming region.

THE CAUSES FOR THE GREAT INCREASE IN THE POPULATION OF CITIES

over that of the country at large are almost too evident to need to be stated. The railroad and telegraph have changed the relations of communities, and have virtually annihilated time and space, and made communication with the great cities so convenient to the rural districts, that the country tavern and the country stores have lost their local attractions and are rapidly disappearing, because the farmer who lives one or two hundred miles away, can seat himself in a comfortable car, and while enjoying his newspaper, glide away to the city, buy his groceries and dry goods, and return with the loss of less time than was occupied in the old-fashioned trip to the village, half a dozen miles from his country home. The itinerant agent of the city merchant makes a market for the products of the soil almost upon the fields where they grow; and when gathered they are hurried away by the express freight train to the city for distribution. The wife and daughter study the fashions at home and do their shopping in the distant city where the variety of goods is unlimited. The great superiority of the institutions of learning, and the

attractions of music, libraries, fine arts and amuse-
ments in the city are drawing from the country
large portions of all classes, especially the more
wealthy, who desire for themselves and their children intelligent recreation and the best educational
advantages. Every year adds to the city new
modes and conveniences for living. In this regard
a degree of personal comfort is secured which cannot be enjoyed in the country. The inventive mind
of man will not be less active in the future than it
has been in the past; and by constant additions to
the conveniences and comforts of living, the allure-
ments and attractions of city life are likely to grow
still stronger with every passing year.

A very intelligent writer in the *Journal of Social
Science*, Mr. Olmstead, now President of the Board
of Central Park Commissioners, and to whom I am
indebted for many important facts, says:

"Experiments indicate that it is possible to send
heated air through a town in pipes, like water, and
that it may be drawn, and the heat which is taken
measured and paid for according to quantity
required."

A bill * has been before us and enacted during
the present session, for the incorporation of a company which proposes to generate steam at some
central point and send it through pipes, in a similar manner, to all who desire it, so that one only
needs to turn a faucet to set the culinary depart-

* Senate Document No. 37.

ment of the domestic establishment in full operation without loss of time or the annoyances incident to starting fires.

Mr. Olmstead again says: "It is plain that we have scarcely begun to turn to account the advantages offered to towns-people in the electric telegraph; we really have not made a beginning with those offered in the pneumatic tube, though their substantial character has been fully demonstrated. By the use of these two instruments a tradesman ten miles away on the other side of a city, may be communicated with, and goods obtained from him by a housekeeper, as quickly and with as little personal inconvenience as if he were in the next block. A single tube station for five hundred families, acoustic pipes for the transmission of orders to it from each house, with a carrier service for local distribution of packages, is all that is needed for this purpose."*

This is not mere sentimental speculation, Mr. President, for just such conveniences are now in successful operation in some of the cities of Europe, which are far in advance of American cities in other labor-saving and economical contrivances. Every invention for cultivating the soil and harvesting and marketing its productions,—which enables one man to do the work of five,—sends four families into the city. A moment's reflection as to

* See Appendix for Prof. Holton's views upon the subject of compressed air.

what has been accomplished in the last twenty
years, in the line of such improvements alone, will
enable us to anticipate indefinite progress in this
direction in the future, until the country districts
will need only farm laborers and engineers to
operate the machinery which will perform the bulk
of the work that is to be done. There can be no
doubt, therefore, of the tendency, and the causes
thereof, of the people of all civilized nations to
congregate in great cities.

A glance only at a few facts connected with this
fruitful topic is all that is possible here. But I can
safely say, there can hardly be a more important
subject presented for your consideration, or that of
legislators, state and national, throughout the entire
country, than that which relates to the inevitably
rapid growth in the population and wealth of large
cities. It is not a temporary inclination of the times,
for the causes producing it are as self-evident as
sunlight, and there can be no reaction until books,
newspapers, schools, churches, and all sources of
knowledge shall be blotted out and the people de-
generate into the condition of barbarism. Hence,
I repeat, that a wise foresight will lose no time in
making suitable preparation for this characteristic of
the age. Ample territory should be embraced within
the boundaries of a municipal power which will
carefully consider and mature comprehensive plans,
and establish the lines of its avenues, streets, squares
and parks, making provision for health, convenience

and beauty, while it can be done at small cost, and done in such manner, too, that the people may know that they are not in a few years to be heavily taxed, as they now are, to correct the errors which a little timely reflection on the part of their law-makers would have rendered wholly unnecessary.

Among other important measures recently introduced into the legislature of the state of New York, is one providing for the annexation of some eight miles square of the lower end of Westchester County to the city of New York. This will make the city more than sixteen miles long, and will add immensely, not only to its population, but to the value of its real estate, especially in the upper portion, lying contiguous to the new quarter. The two great bridges now building across the East River will ultimately bring Brooklyn, Long Island City, Astoria, and a number of other Long Island towns within its limits.*

Now, sir, the first conditions to be provided for in planning the future growth of Boston, are the health, the safety, the protection of property, and the education, morality and prosperity of its inhabitants; and the first and most important duty is to

PROVIDE FOR THE HEALTH OF THE PEOPLE,

for without health, wealth and all earthly attractions vanish, and life itself becomes a burden.

* Since these remarks were made this measure has become a law.

No one doubts but that the Boston of to-day is
but a nucleus of an immense city, that will extend
hereafter over miles of the rural territory adjoining
its present limits. He who looks into the future can
see it with as much certainty as though it were now
in existence. Neither will it be disputed that the
average life of mankind in the compact portions of
large cites is very much less than in the country, or
in localities where sunshine and air have free circulation, and the foliage of trees and shrubbery is
abundant. We have only to turn to the records
of the scientific institutions upon this crowded peninsula to learn that, in the closely built portions of
a city, "a given quantity of air contains considerably less of the elements which must be received
through the lungs, than the air of the country, or
the air which is purified by foliage in the open places
in the city; and that, instead of being healthful, it
carries into the lungs highly corrupt and irritating
matters, the action of which tends strongly to viti-
ate the sources of vigor." So marked are these in-
dications, that metallic substances corrode and wear
away under the atmospheric influences in cities and
towns that are compactly built, while they are but
slightly affected in the pure air of the country, or
in open spaces or around parks.

Even in the time of Alexander the value of long,
straight and broad streets, as ventilators of a city,
were understood; but four centuries later, the
founders of London laid out that city in such a

manner that those who followed them, a dozen centuries after, found that the way in which it had been done was the cause of an amount of misery and waste of life and property which was appalling even to the civilization of the seventeenth century. They had no plan, and were governed by no law of the elements or of man, but proceeded, as Boston has done, in a desultory, "helter-skelter" manner of building upon accidental paths. They provided no squares, or parks, or breathing places,—their streets were narrow and crooked; and the results were sadly obvious in after-time.* About every forty years, on an average, from 1318 to 1666, the city was scourged with plagues and devastating epidemics. On each of these dreadful occasions all of the people who had adequate means moved into the open suburbs to escape the destroyer. Now and then a conflagration would sweep away acres of buildings, and thus open "breathing places" which purified the atmosphere and restored health to the surrounding population. Still they went on building as before, not heeding the lessons of their experience any more than Boston heeds her own, until the period of the great plague in 1665, when the march of fatality through their narrow thoroughfares

---

* "Streets were by preference narrow and crooked. Houses might crowd against each other, and encroach upon the streets, and throw out overhanging balconies and oriels and turrets, and rise to the height of a dozen stories, until the threadlike alleys below were completely shut in from sunlight. But with the city wall once built, no lateral expansion was possible for generations, or perhaps for centuries. These were the haunts of the mediæval pestilences."—*Bacon.*

was so sweeping that the living were not numerous
enough to bury the dead; and more than one hundred thousand citizens of London were hurried into
eternity in a single year. And then, as if the unseen Power intended to make the warning against
the violations of natural laws in the construction of
their city still more impressive, the following year
four hundred and thirty-six acres of the crowded
city, covering four hundred streets, and embracing
thirteen thousand dwellings, were converted into
ashes in a few hours by the flames of a single conflagration. What a sacrifice was this to the Moloch
of ignorance and human folly! The lesson which
it teaches is still before us, unlearned, and may yet
be studied with benefit to the civilization of the
nineteenth century.

Then it was, before the fire was yet subdued,
that the great and distinguished architect, Sir
Christopher Wren, prepared an economical and
simple plan for avoiding former evils in the construction of the city. His recommendations were
promptly approved by the king and the wise and
reflecting men of his time; yet the difficulties of
equalizing and adjusting benefits and damages
among the owners of the land were so great, that
the improvements sought to be introduced were
but partially adopted, and these at an enormous
cost to the tax-payers of the unfortunate city. Do
Senators remember whether any part of this history
has been recently, and is now being repeated in

Boston? And if the terrific admonitions of history
have failed to impress the local community with the
necessity of at least attempting, in the interest of
ethical duties and social happiness, to apply a
remedy, cannot something in the way of state legislation be suggested or adopted, which, all other
means having failed, will appeal to popular selfish-
ness by demonstrating it to be for the *pecuniary*
interests of the people, to no longer plan as if the
duration of this world and all happiness was to ter-
minate with the brief period of their own lives.

Mankind has, however, gained something from
the terrors of the pestilence that nearly depopu-
lated London in the seventeenth century. It was
discovered that the people who fled to the open
country beyond the city limits were not affected by
the dread disease, and therefore those who could
afford the means reserved open spaces around their
dwellings. The more wealthy located their dwellings around an open field, where trees were planted
and shrubs and flowers were cultivated. Squares
and parks were thus introduced, and London now
has more than four thousand acres where sunlight
and air and foliage have uninterrupted freedom to
perform their beneficent mission of dispelling the
miasms that arise from the more crowded sections of the thronged city. Since these progressive steps were taken, no plague has visited the
great metropolis.

But we are in the midst of home events and
6

facts whose teaching are not less important and
striking. In order to ascertain the comparative
mortality of various quarters of the city of Boston,
Dr. George Derby, the very able and efficient Sec-
retary of the State Board of Health, in 1870 divided the city into twenty-four health districts, each
comprising either an entire ward or part of a ward,
or parts of two or three wards—the objects of this
division being to group together a population similarly situated as to the conveniences and comforts
of life,—those in the best circumstances in separate
districts from those living in unwholesome dwellings, and in circumstances of comparative destitu-
tion. Each district contained, as far as possible, a
population similarly situated as to surroundings,
and conveniences of living.

The population of each district, at all ages, was
obtained through the census, taken in 1870, by per-
mission of the United States government, and the
deaths at all ages in each district, for the same year,
were obtained from records at the City Hall. With
these elements some very striking results were obtained, which were published in the Second Annual
Report of the State Board of Health. For instance, the death-rate (i. e. the annual number of
deaths to every 10,000 of population) varies from
57 in the most favored district, to 379 in the most
unhealthy,—a difference of nearly *seven to one!*
The smaller ratio of mortality just named, 57, was
in the new Back Bay territory, west of Common-

wealth Avenue, and adjacent to the Public Garden, the Common and the broad avenues where sunlight and air and the foliage of trees are most abundant. In Roxbury Highlands, the next most favored locality, the ratio was 91, and in the district covering the Back Bay east of Commonwealth Avenue, it was 98 to each 10,000 living.

It was 142 in the east half of ward eleven, 152 in the district comprising the best part of ward four, and 156 on the south side of Beacon Hill, including Beacon, Mt. Vernon and Pinckney streets. In ward sixteen (Dorchester) the death-rate was 163.

The foregoing may all be considered as the more favored localities, for the deaths are *less* than the average mortality of the state, which for the last seven years was 176 in 10,000.

We come next to districts in which the mortality *exceeded* the just quoted mortality of the state. In the Suffolk Street district the mortality was 177 to each 10,000; in East Boston, 187; in ward fourteen, 188; in ward eight, 195; in ward ten, 201; also in the Church Street district, 201.

But in the regions filled with a foreign-born population, crowded into tenement houses in narrow streets, and otherwise living under conditions less eligible than in the districts already named, we find the death-rate surely and rapidly increasing. In South Boston, the rate averages about 256 in 10,000; in ward thirteen, 253; in ward four,

about Portland Street (formerly the old mill pond),
267; in the South Cove land, in ward seven, 273.

The mortality at the North End, the most
thickly settled part of the city, is still greater. In
ward two, it was 296. This is exceeded only by
one district in the city—the most unhealthy of all
—namely, in the low lands of ward fifteen, which
are inhabited by a mixed population. The death-
rate here was enormous, being 379 in 10,000. The
mortality among infants varies exceedingly with
the location and surroundings, and forms a very
large part of the mortality.

In a district including a part of ward four, *nearly
half* of the whole number of infants died (to be
explained in part, however, by the existence of an
infantile boarding-house therein).

In the South Boston districts, and in the district
inhabited by the colored population, more than
one-third of the infants died. But in Roxbury
Highlands, where the total deaths were 91 in
10,000 only, the mortality among infants was *less
than one-tenth*, a difference of nearly five to one,
as compared with ward four, where the population
is most dense.

"The death-rates of East Boston and the North
End," says Dr. Derby, "present a contrast which
is worthy of examination. These districts are of
nearly equal population, and the numbers at all
ages very nearly correspond, yet the mortality in
one is half as great again as in the other. One is

crowded, in great part deprived of sunlight; the other has abundance of light and air." "Can a stronger argument," he says, "be offered in favor of providing breathing spaces for the people?"

In the towns and cities proposed for union with Boston, the average number of deaths for seven years was only 155 in 10,000, while in Boston and Charlestown combined they were 209½, showing the deaths to be nearly 30 per cent. less in the more open adjoining towns than in the two crowded cities.

Thus, from authentic calculations, the causes which promote a high degree of public health, and the causes which produce disease, sickness and death, have been clearly shown, and it is proved that both are largely within human control. From the unquestionable authority adduced, it will also appear to what extent the municipal power of a city is responsible, not only for the comfort and happiness, but for the health and lives of its population; for it has been demonstrated, by uncontrovertible facts, that where ample territory is available the city can be made, if properly laid out and cared for, and subject to one power and one system of government, even more healthy than the average of country life.* In the broad avenues and in the streets that border on the Common and the

* "It is clear that the great city of the future is to be a place where life is as long and as secure as anywhere else, and where physical development and health is as great in degree, however it may differ in kind, from that of the agricultural regions."—*Prof. Francis Bacon.*

little Public Garden adjoining it, the annual deaths
average only fifty-seven in 10,000, while in the
whole state the average is 176, or three times as
great.   In other portions of the city, *not less favorably located*, but which have not been permitted
to enjoy the health-giving advantages nature has
provided for all, the deaths are 379 in 10,000, or
nearly *seven hundred* per cent. larger than in the
open and cleanly localities.

Now, Mr. President, if the death-rate in a considerable portion of a city is very much less than
the average in the whole state, shall it be said that
under the lead of modern science, the people refuse to secure the means for maintaining at least
an equal degree of health in those portions of the
city that are to be *hereafter* constructed?   Is human
life so cheap that the law-makers will disregard
these facts?   Yet, when it is proposed to initiate a
step that makes it easy to secure such result it is
characterized as "sentimentalism" or "speculation."

Sir, there are some so wrapped in ideas of speculation that they think of no other rule by which
to measure the motives and actions of others but
that which governs themselves, and, unlike Macbeth,
behold it even in the vacant eyes of the walking
nightmare that haunts their vision of gain,—those
who, measuring life and duty by the rule of dollars
and cents, would, if they had the power, bottle up
the free air of heaven, and retail it to a gasping
public for a pecuniary consideration.

"Speculation" lies not at the foundation of this plan, but may follow those who favor annexation in a most objectionable form,—the piecemeal process— that diverts legislation from the greater good of the masses to the aid of the few who would concentrate in particular localities the benefits arising therefrom; thus delaying and therefore doubling and trebling the cost of those essential public improvements which should be accomplished only upon the basis of an equality of benefits among all the communities whose situation, with reference to the subject, is substantially the same. The object of legislation is justice, and the promotion of the greatest good for the greatest number; and upon this theory it becomes the duty of the state to interpose its power in shaping the future of its metropolis, so that the best interests of all its citizens may be promoted.

The propositions embraced in the Resolve have to do with the serious business of providing not only for the prosperity and comfort of millions of people who are to come after us, but for the prevention, also, of a useless sacrifice of life and health.

I commend to legislators, whose duty it is to guard the public welfare, some startling facts developed in the report of the Board of Health of the present year, which has just been laid upon Senators' desks. If it shall be found that the death-rate, independent of the increase arising from

the small-pox epidemic, is twenty-five per cent.
larger than the preceding year, there is a cause
for it; and it is for them to say whether the proper
sanitary condition of the city can be restored and
protected *short* of a complete reorganization of the
system of drainage and surface improvements in
the territory entirely surrounding the present limits
of Boston. An improved system of drainage will
be one great remedy for existing evils; another
and more complete one may be found in the establishment of

PARKS, SQUARES, AND BROAD AVENUES,

which are essential to the preservation of health in
all great cities.* An intelligent writer and excellent authority, in commenting upon the necessity as
well as difficulties of making suitable provisions for
securing the health of the people who are rapidly
filling up the great cities of the world, says : " Air
is disinfected by sunlight and foliage. Foliage also
acts mechanically to purify the air by screening it.
Opportunity and inducement to escape at frequent

* An eminent physician in New York City, in speaking of the influence
of Central Park in promoting public health, says :—

"Where I formerly ordered patients of a certain class to give up their
business altogether and go out of town, I now often advise simply mod-
eration, and prescribe a ride in the park before going to their offices, and
again a drive with their families before dinner. By simply adopting this
course as a habit, men who have been breaking down frequently re-
cover tone rapidly, and are able to retain an active and controlling influence in an important business, from which they would have otherwise
been forced to retire. I direct school-girls, under certain circumstances,
to be taken wholly, or in part, from their studies, and sent to spend several hours a day rambling on foot in the park."

intervals from the confined and vitiated air of the commercial quarters, and to supply with air screened and purified by trees, and recently acted upon by the sunlight, together with opportunity and inducements to escape from conditions requiring vigilance, wariness and activity toward other men, if these could be economically supplied, our problem," he says, "would be solved."

There is no locality where all the conditions so abundantly exist for solving the problems that are now being discussed in connection with the growth of cities, as in Boston and vicinity. That they have not been long since solved here, and Boston placed in the front rank of the healthiest and most beautiful cities in the world, is because the people have not accepted the offers presented by the generous hand of nature.

It is of the highest importance to preserve within the limits of a city, for purposes of health and beauty, as much of nature as possible. Trees, shrubs, and flowers were created for highest usefulness, and, wherever permitted, are constantly at work in the service of man ; and whenever man attempts to exclude nature and her laws from his plans, he is sure to do it at a costly penalty. Light, a free circulation of air, and the purifying influence of foliage, are now admitted to be indispensable requisites to public health. To have these in abundance in the residential portions of a city, there must

7

be broad avenues, with broad sidewalks, lined with vigorous shade-trees.*

There must also be open spaces or parks where men, women and children can indulge in those recreative sports and enjoyments that conduce so much to the health, vigor, morality and manliness of the people ; and these parks should, if possible, contain sheets of water where sailing, rowing and other aquatic enjoyments can be freely indulged in by all classes of people.† There should, also, be numerous bathing-places to promote cleanliness, and, therefore, godliness.

Observe the location of city school-houses, four or five stories high, crowded into narrow streets, where neither sunlight nor pure air can reach them. At recess, when the pupils are allowed a few moments to escape the confined atmosphere of the building, they are sent out out into "pens," enclosed by high walls and paved with brick.   Sir, I will venture the opinion that from two to five years would be added to the average life of the native population of cities, and the mortality among school-children be largely reduced, if public educational structures were required to be built not more than two stories high, and each located upon a two-or-three-acre park.   And then, if fewer hours of study,

* The length of the paved streets in Paris is about 340 miles ; 225 miles of these streets were, previous to the siege of the city by the Prussian army in 1870, lined with trees, gardens and planted squares.

† Cricket and base-ball clubs are accommodated in most of the London parks, and swimming is permitted in the lakes at certain hours.

and more hours of out-door physical exercise were required, a more handsome, vigorous, healthy and intelligent race of men and women would surely follow. No higher service could be rendered the state and humanity than an effort to accomplish such a result, which is only possible where there is ample territorial area under the control of one system of governmental authority.

A dozen broad avenues from * 125 to 200 feet wide radiating in different directions from the compact portions of Boston, through the territory which it is proposed to unite with it, should have been constructed years ago, so that the country air, ever fresh and pure, from the green hills beyond, could sweep without interruption to the crowded marts of commerce. Near deep water and the railway

---

* The Avenue de l'Imperatrice, in Paris, leading to the Bois de Boulogne, is bordered by continuous gardens; inside are carriage-roads, and beyond gardens and alleys. Its width, 429 feet, is thus distributed:—

Carriage-way,	.	50 feet.
Footpath, on one side,	.	36 "
Horsepath, on the other side,	.	36 "
Grass and shrubbery, .	.	87 "
" " "	.	87 "
Iron railing.		
2 small streets, on each side of which four sidewalks, 20 feet,		61 "
Iron railing.		
To line of houses,	.	36 "
" "	.	36 "
		———
Total, .	.	429 "

The width of the Avenue Neuilly is, .	.	231 "
" " " " Vincennes is,	.	231 "
" " " new Boulevard Malsherbes is,	.	195 "

There are 21 or 22 of these broad boulevards in Paris. They vary much in width, but nowhere are they less than the preceding.

centres, where the bulk of trade must be carried on,
broad avenues are not practicable, and perhaps
not desirable, except an occasional one, as great
thoroughfares or outlets from the more crowded
localities. Such, however, with an occasional square
in the business sections, are indispensable, not only
as "breathing-places," but as checks to the spread
of great conflagrations. Values to the amount of
$100,000,000 were consumed in the fiery blast of a
few hours' duration in November last ; and let me
say, just here, it might have been two or three or
four hundred millions but for the accidental existence of one small open space, which the battling
firemen could safely trust to check the march of the
storm of flame in that direction, while they could
marshal their forces and interpose a united will
against its spread in other directions. The remem-
brance of the spot where stood historic old Fort
Hill ought to be an ever-present witness here and
in the Municipal Council Chamber to remind us all
of the priceless value of an occasional square and
broad street, even in the commercial quarters of a
great city. These cannot be secured without ample
territorial area under the control of a single municipal power.

These are the outlines of the essentials, as every-
body will agree, for the foundations of a great city;
and they are all embraced within the territory which
it is now propsed to unite under one government.

Land upon this territory to the amount of at least

three thousand acres should be secured as park reservations, so located in *different portions* of it, as to be conveniently accessible to the people. The municipal authorities of nearly all the large cities of the world now admit their irreparable error in securing park lands too late to bring them as near to the centre of population as they ought to be for public recreation and health. Their mistakes should teach us wisdom. When this is done the entire territory should as speedily as possible be laid out into squares, avenues, streets and boulevards, and the lines permanently established, so that the future of the territory and the plans for its improvement could be correctly understood. There would then be ample opportunity for the exercise of public taste in the selection of locations for residential improvements, and the moment the lines were established, the plans for private construction would necessarily conform to them.

It is estimated that the income accruing from the rise and increase of taxable property would more than pay for all expenditures necessary for laying water-pipes, draining, grading, constructing streets and improving and beautifying the parks; for work upon these would be prosecuted only as fast as private construction would demand.

The establishment of Central Park, New York, was the result of a legislative mistake. No such magnificent work was at first intended; and when the plans of the commissioners, who happened to

be excellent men, were made known, they were
denounced by the authorities, the press, and the
public generally, and, during the first three years
of their service, they were caricatured and ridiculed
on all sides, and, as you will remember, were once
or twice mobbed. But they pushed on rapidly,
working, for a time, night and day, in order to attain so much progress that the work could not be
stopped. To-day there is not a voter in New York
City who would not, if necessary, imperil his life to
prevent that great work from being undone. Owing
to the original barrenness of the land, the cost of
Central Park has, from its origin, been large,—being
nearly $12,500,000, including cost of land, up to
the present time. Not taking into account its
invaluable contributions to the health and pleasure
of the people, it has more than paid for itself from
the income of taxable property which it has created
around it, and the city now receives from this source
an annual income of $2,726,595, after paying in-
terest on the total cost of land and all improvements
up to this date. And yet it has but few of the
natural attractions and advantages for economical
construction which exist on the territory around
Boston, and which is also much nearer the heart
of population: the northern boundary of Central
Park is eight miles from Wall Street, while the
reservations here need not average more than
four miles from the State House.

The advance in value of real estate around the

park has been at the rate of 200 per cent. per annum.* It is also estimated by the commissioners that the entire cost of the park has been much more than repaid by the additional capital drawn to the city through its influence. About ten million people annually visit the park, and yet there is not one steam railroad reaching its boundaries, while there are twelve or fourteen different steam roads extending through the territory which it is proposed to unite with Boston, where parks would undoubtedly be laid out, should it be under the jurisdiction of one municipality.

Sir, are improvements such as I have attempted to describe, and which will promote the health, prosperity and all the higher elements of society and good government, desirable in connection with the growth of the metropolis of Massachusetts and New England? If so, can they be successfully inaugurated without placing over all the cities and towns on this territory a government which will unite the scattered interests of the people under one homogeneous municipal power? A negative answer may be inferred,—first, because though there are now nearly half a million people residing on this territory, no such improvements exist; and, second, because Boston is behind, far behind every

* "Land immediately about the park, the frontage on it being seven miles in length, instead of taking the course anticipated by those opposed to the policy of the commission, has advanced in value at the rate of two hundred per cent. per annum."—F. L. Olmstead, President Board Central Park Commissioners, Journal Social Science, 1871, p. 35.

other large modern city in securing them; and, to
her dishonor be it said, has never added any park
grounds to the " Old Common " which the residents
of the little village of Boston reserved for themselves more than two hundred years ago. New
York has eleven hundred and Philadelphia more
than three thousand acres of park grounds.

Now, sir, while the interests of these sixteen
municipalities are identical and centered in one
locality, they seek prosperity under independent
governments. If the owner of a fine ship should
load that ship with a valuable cargo for a trading
venture, and place sixteen captains on board with
equal powers, directed to go where in their judgment they could realize the greatest success, there
would, of course, be a mutiny among them before
she left her moorings, and the enterprise would
fail until there was a consolidation of authority,
and, under command of a single power, her course
should be fixed and her sails spread to the breeze
that would speed her on a prosperous voyage.
Human nature is the same on the land as on the
sea,—the same among different local governments
as among different men,—and no plan for a comprehensive system of improvements among this
cluster of municipalities upon a scale at all com-
mensurate with the demands of their population,
can be projected without coming in contact with
local jealousies and conflicting ideas and interests
which hinder the progress of all.

Charles-river Basin, for instance, which is bounded by Boston, Cambridge and Brookline, is susceptible of improvements which would eclipse in beauty the celebrated embankments upon the Thames River in London, and could be accomplished at a fraction of the expense. Will Boston begin the improvements? No! not without a satisfactory arrangement with Cambridge. Will Cambridge and Brookline undertake the much-needed enterprise? Certainly not, unless Boston is a willing partner in the expense. One city is not going to tax its people to benefit another city, if it can avoid it. Well, suppose they could all agree to share an equitable proportion of the expense? Can they then agree as to what that equitable proportion is—the amount to be expended, and the style and particular characteristics of the improvement? There is no prospect of such harmony until human nature is re-organized and made fit to participate in the joys of the distant millennium; for the residents of Cambridge, most of whom do business in Boston, would be first taxed at home for that city's proportion of the expense,—then they would have to pay another tax upon their merchandise and real estate in Boston for that city's proportion of the expense; so that a resident of Cambridge would be obliged to pay two taxes, while a resident of Boston would pay but one. Is this fact likely to contribute to the harmony of their calculations? As a large proportion of the

8

taxes collected in Boston are paid by residents of
other towns that would not be benefited by an expenditure of which they would have to bear a considerable part, of course all such improvements and
the legislation necessary to authorize them, would
have to encounter their hostility. And the result
would be that Charles-river Basin would remain
in the future, as in the past, though in the heart
of an immense population, a continued disgrace
to their intelligence, taste and enterprise.

This case is an illustration of a principle which
will apply to all other 'localities under consideration.

Who has not, for years past, heard of the "Mil-
ler-river nuisance," the stench arising from which
has been strong enough to breed a pestilence in
the neighborhood surrounding it? The odors from
this nest of putrefaction are so intense in the hot
months, that passengers in railroad trains passing
through it are obliged to hold their breath and
pinch their noses until the poisoned atmosphere is
passed. It is still there, however, undisturbed.
Why? Because it lies on the borders of three
cities,—Cambridge, Somerville and Charlestown.
Can it be supposed that it would have been
permitted to remain where life and health were
imperiled by its existence, if it had been subject
to the control of one municipal power?

But we are told that Boston has territory enough
now, though shapeless and circumscribed, to ac-

commodate her growth. That is not true, because
nearly half of her business men reside outside of
her limits. There may be acres enough to accommodate them; but there is no power in a republic
that can force the growth of a city in any particular
direction. Look at the map which is now before
you, and see how absurd such a suggestion appears. Its growth will be governed by natural
causes over which man has no control. His duty
is limited to using and developing the advantages
which nature presents. Where did the idea obtain
that the area of a city was to be confined to particular limits when there were no natural barriers
to define them? Why insist upon confining the
great population of Boston to a territorial area
less than half as large as many of the towns in the
state which have a population of only two or three
thousand? County and town lines should be
treated as mere fictions when they become a bar to
public benefits. I have tried to believe that the
object of government was to provide for the
public welfare; and if that could be better served
by making the boundary lines of a city ten miles
square instead of one mile square, then the duties
of a legislator were determined and clear.

Now, let us see in which direction the current
of population is setting about Boston. The following table, prepared from the census of 1870,
shows that the percentage of increase in the four
northern adjoining cities and towns of Revere,

Malden, Somerville and Cambridge was 43 per
cent. in five years, while in the four southern adjoining towns of Dorchester, Roxbury, Brookline
and Brighton, where endeavors are being made to
force the population by piecemeal-annexation, the
increase in five years was 22 per cent., while in
Boston, as it existed *before* the annexation of Roxbury and Dorchester, the increase was but *five* per
cent.; thus exhibiting the fact which I desire to
impress upon your memory that the population in
the adjoining towns is increasing several hundred
per cent. faster than in old Boston.

	Population in 1865.	Population in 1870.	Increase in 5 years, 1865-70.	Per cent. Increase in 5 years, 1865-70.	Per cent. 10 years, 1850-60.	Per cent. 10 years, 1855-65.
Boston, exclusive of Dorchester and Roxbury,	192,318	203,479	11,161	5.80	29.92	19.83
Dorchester (16th ward),	10,717	12,261	1,514	14.41	22.50	28.50
Roxbury (13th, 14th, 15th wards),	28,426	34,773	6,347	22.33	71.24	53.91
Boston, Dorchester and Roxbury,	231,461	250,513	19,052	8.23	30.35	23.53
Chelsea,	11,403	18,547	4,114	28.77	99.89	41.89
Revere,	858	1,197	339	39.51	56.68	8.19
Winthrop,	635	532	—101*	15.96	—	55.63
Arlington,	2,760	3,261	501	18.15	21.29	3.57
Belmont,	1,279	1,513	234	18.30	—	—
Brighton,	3,854	4,967	1,113	28.88	43.25	33.19
Cambridge,	29,112	39,634	10,522	36.14	71.27	42.19
Charlestown,	26,399	28,323	1,924	7.29	45.59	21.61
Everett,	6,840 {	2,220 }	2,747	40.17	66.10	48.93
Malden,		7,367				
Medford,	4,839	5,717	878	18.14	28.86	5.13
Somerville,	9,353	14,685	5,332	57.01	129.67	61.09
Watertown,	3,779	4,326	547	14.17	15.26	5.02
Brookline,	5,262	6,650	1,388	26.23	105.24	40.81
West Roxbury,	6,912	8,683	1,771	25.62	—	43.64
Total 15 towns above,	116,283	147,622	31,339	26.95	—	—
Boston and all 17 towns above,	347,744	398,135	50,391	14.39	—	—
Franklin County,	31,340	32,635	1,295	4.13	1.83	—.49*

* Loss.

COMMUNICATION BETWEEN BOSTON AND THE NORTH
BANK OF CHARLES RIVER

is becoming a very important subject for consideration. Opinions are entertained by many, that the
area of Boston should not extend across this river,
and that appropriate provision can be made for the
rapid increase of population by the existence of *two*
cities—one on the north and another on the south
of it. It is difficult to discover the reasons for
such a conclusion; for the cleanest, healthiest, best
governed and best drained cities in the world—
like London, Paris, St. Petersburg. Berlin, Vienna,
Glasgow and others, embrace both banks of a
river—and, in most civilized countries, it has
become a settled conviction that a river should not
be the boundary line of a city, especially where
both banks are equally favorable for occupation
and improvement. It is evident that an extensive
system of bridges must be maintained across the
Charles River, because the population is becoming
dense on both sides of it; and in a few years there
will be hundreds of thousands residing upon the
northern banks, who, in pursuit of their vocations
will be obliged to cross daily to the south side
where the great centre of business near the deep
waters of the harbor will ever exist. The bridges,
therefore, must be ample, and, in their construction, free from parsimonious influences. Where
bridges are necessary they ought to be among the

most imposing, beautiful and attractive architectural features of a great city; and the future promises an extensive field here for the exercise of skill in the art of bridge building in connection with improvements in the "Charles-river Basin"; for every bridge between Boston and the north bank of the river, except those crossed by railroads, will have to be "reconstructed" and enlarged in a few years, to accommodate the growing demands of the public.

Each of the several independent municipalities with which these different bridges connect, endeavors to avoid as much as possible the expense and responsibility of their construction and care,—and inasmuch as the channel and boundary line which separate these governments, runs close to the Boston shore, the chief expense of maintaining these long bridges falls upon the weakest municipality. Therefore, unless both ends of these public structures are under the control of a single power, the bridges of Boston are not likely to rank with those of London and Paris, which are the pride of every beholder.

The fact is, the bridges about Boston, viewing them in the light of usefulness and beauty,—reflect no credit upon those who designed and planned their construction. They are a source of legislative controversy every year—and are far, very far, from being adequate to a proper accommodation of the public; and thus they will remain

until they are subject to the management of one
instead of many governments.

COST OF DELAY IN UNITING BOSTON WITH THE CITIES AND TOWNS AROUND IT.

Mr. President, it is admitted by the opponents
of this measure that the union of these cities and
towns must take place at some time, but they think
the effort to accomplish it now is premature.

There is no one who would not regard it as very
absurd to attempt to maintain independent municipal governments, with coördinate powers, in each
of the sixteen wards of Boston where there is but
one common interest. Senators can readily im-
agine the turmoil and local jealousies that would
follow where each had the power to place a check
upon the progress of the other. Now, the different cities and towns under consideration bear nearly the same relation to-day toward Boston and each
other as do the various wards of Boston, and when
the population is as numerous—as it will be in a
very few years—will it be less absurd to attempt to
maintain an independent government over each of
these sixteen cities and towns, while their individual and combined interests are so fused as
to make them practically but one community?
The proposition answers itself.

If, therefore, the consolidation of these governments is to be accomplished at all, with a view
to general public improvements which shall be in

keeping with the spirit of the time, and with the
intelligence of Massachusetts, it should be done
immediately, for the cost of delay, as has been
shown in the past history of Boston, is simply enormous. I will illustrate this by giving the valuation of 1861 and 1872, showing the increase in
values in a period of only eleven years in the cities
and towns which it is now proposed to unite. The
facts in the following table will be found particularly interesting upon this point.

9

A Table showing the Comparative Valuation of certain Cities and Towns in the Commonwealth for the Years 1861 and 1872.

TOWNS.	1861 Personal.	1861 Real.	1861 Total Valuation.	1872 Personal.	1872 Real.	1872 Total Valuation.
Arlington,	$865,190	$1,671,926	$2,679,366	$1,697,122	$2,685,994	$5,383,323
Belmont,	829,813	1,300,663	2,130,476	878,110	2,180,371	3,368,484
Brighton,	1,680,150	2,206,817	3,895,287	2,358,976	8,562,645	10,881,621
Cambridge,	6,171,700	15,511,000	21,682,700	26,033,450	39,214,980	45,218,350
Everett,* }	575,110	2,820,260	3,395,670	2,089,796	8,795,075	10,884,901
Malden, }						
Medford,	1,759,670	3,413,421	5,183,091	2,527,827	4,792,265	7,320,092
Somerville,	722,100	5,055,500	5,777,600	3,199,860	19,258,165	22,255,325
Watertown,	1,073,404	1,606,700	2,680,300	3,063,140	1,408,970	6,472,110
Brookline,	5,901,000	5,009,100	10,910,100	11,629,311	17,781,600	29,113,911
West Roxbury,	3,082,500	7,401,100	8,187,000	7,123,340	15,381,800	22,505,140
Chelsea,	731,525	6,477,569	7,229,091	2,161,493	14,635,850	16,797,343
Revere,	101,025	662,675	757,300	160,300	1,441,925	1,602,285
Winthrop,	118,686	293,978	362,664	52,650	618,015	671,405
Total,	$23,821,419	$51,300,108	$75,129,518	$22,595,278	$140,781,712	$193,876,990
Boston,	$108,075,000	$167,682,100	$275,760,100	$219,519,050	$364,896,550	$384,115,600
Charlestown,	3,005,100	12,405,400	15,408,500	9,725,320	25,186,800	31,912,102
Total,	$111,081,100	$180,087,500	$291,168,600	$229,301,370	$390,083,350	$889,372,720
Roxbury,	$5,279,000	$15,680,100	$20,962,100	$12,237,700	$53,675,700	$865,913,100
Dorchester,	1,042,500	7,615,400	11,658,100	7,631,100	25,741,200	31,884,300
Total,	$6,321,500	$23,295,500	$32,627,500	$19,861,800	$78,416,900	$898,868,700

* Included in Malden in 1861.

It thus appears that in 1861 the total valuation of
the real and personal property was $366,297,113.
In 1872 it was $911,042,410, showing the astonish-
ing increase in eleven years of $544,745,292, or
about 150 per cent. The value of the real estate
property in 1861 was $231,387,608, and in 1872 had
increased to $609,251,902, or considerably more
than 150 per cent. As park reservations, squares,
avenues, and streets are to come out of the real
property, an adequate estimate of the stupendous
cost of delaying such improvements may be obtained.
But it is not alone in the increased value of real
estate that the danger and cost of delay comes.
There are streets now being laid out and built upon
in these towns and cities which are suggested by
old cart-paths and rights of way,—as was the case
in Boston two hundred years ago,—that are twenty-
five, thirty, and thirty-five feet wide, and upon land,
too, several feet below the grade of proper drainage, after the style of the Church-street district.
These, in a few years, after life and health have
been sacrificed, will have to be widened and the
grades raised, when the land is worth one hundred
times more than it now is,—besides the additional
cost of demolishing and rebuilding structures.

In considering the subject of providing room for
public improvements I omit Old Boston and Charlestown, because there is no room in them for improvements, unless it is obtained by demolishing structures. Therefore I include Dorchester and Roxbury

—the four new wards—with the other towns proposed for annexation, as the localities where land must be taken for parks and broad avenues. The valuation in these districts in 1861 was $107,757,018. In 1872 it had grown to $291,685,690, showing an average annual increase for a period of eleven years of nearly $17,000,000. From these data any one can determine approximately, what will be the annual cost of delaying those public improvements which the future is sure to demand.

It has been estimated that at least $250,000,000 of additional taxable property would have been created, not merely by enhanced valuation, but drawn here from different parts of the world, if the improvements which have been suggested had been commenced ten years ago, and judiciously prosecuted from that time. This, and the loss of valuable opportunities, which can never be recovered, should be added to other losses arising from procrastination in providing for future necessities, which are as sure to exist as the inevitable coming and going of the tides.

Mr. President, how long will this community—renowned for its economical, money-making propensities, as well as for its liberality—continue to sacrifice, not only the comforts and luxuries which nature has so abundantly spread before them, but at the same time cleave to the policy which belittles their intelligence, and, while creating no new sources of wealth or improvement, forces upon the people expenditures so stupendous as hardly to be determined by the problems of arithmetic. Is it not time that the legislative power of the Commonwealth had measured its duties and obligations toward the people of her metropolis and those that cluster about it? But we are told that a union of these cities and towns under one government would be productive of a dangerous

CENTRALIZATION OF POWER.

What is understood by centralization of power? It is the concentration of power which rightfully belongs to the many in the hands of the few. I admit that, even under our democratic system, there are dangers in this direction against which it is our duty to guard, especially when that power may be lodged in the hands of the few who may abuse it. But the diffusion of this concentrated power among the many, to whom it rightfully belongs, and whose interests are opposed to its abuse, surely cannot be called "centralization"; and that is precisely what is proposed to be accomplished by uniting the several municipalities, named in the Resolve, under one government.

Nearly all the residents of these fifteen cities and towns have their business places in Boston. Here they pay a large proportion of the taxes, and yet they have no voice in the government which they help to support, and to which they are subject. Their interests are, therefore, divided between dif-

ferent municipalities—the one where they domicile
and vote, and the other where they own property
and transact their business; and a divided interest
is always a weak one: neither community having the
benefit of that strength which comes from a unity
of interest and sentiment, so essential among the
people in promoting their own prosperity and the
growth and grandeur of the city of which they con-
stitute a part. The property of the suburban residents, now amounting to between two and three
hundred million dollars, and all the considerations
that attach to it, are also wholly subject to the control of voters within the limits of Boston, a majority
of whom may have nothing at stake which will cause
them to feel any concern as to the quality of the
municipal government beyond what arises from the
exercise of the right of suffrage which is secured to
them by the payment of a simple poll tax. Eighty-
seven per cent. of the voters in some of the wards
of Boston are now of this description.

The property-holders, business men and artisans
who pursue their vocations in Boston and reside beyond its limits, are increasing, as has been shown,
at least one hundred per cent. more rapidly than
those who domicile within the present boundary
lines of the city; and thus, in a few years, they
will have a predominant interest in the business and
property—which contribute largely to the welfare
of the entire State—in the city where they cannot
vote. Therefore, in a few years, the larger interests

and those which require most protection, may be entirely without representation in the municipal power which controls it.

I ask Senators to think seriously upon this subject, and to judge whether the public welfare and the cause of good government in Massachusetts, and especially in her metropolis, does not demand that this power, now lodged in the hands of the few, shall not extend to those to whom the exercise of it rightfully belongs, before the mischief arising from the present incongruous state of affairs shall be irreparable.

Is it in accordance with our organic laws that property to the amount of hundreds of millions of dollars shall be subject to taxation without as far as possible securing to the people from whom it is collected the right of representation in the government imposing such tax? It is not the fault of the business men of Boston that the growth of the city has crowded them beyond its limits. They desire to live where their business is, and be subject to one system and one uniform rate of taxation. They demand this as their right, and it is the duty of the legislature to secure to them this inalienable privilege by extending municipal jurisdiction over territory that shall, for this purpose, afford ample accommodation for all time, and be convenient and suitable for the existence of a city that will keep pace with the advancing civilization of the age. When the legislature has made such provision, then its duties will have been performed, and its responsibilities cease, and not before.

A fear is expressed by some that such an aggregation of population, under a single municipal power, as is proposed by this measure, will increase the danger of

IMMORALITY AND CORRUPTION

in the administration of the affairs of the city. The reasoning that leads to such a fear appears to me to be founded in error,—a palpable error. It is the density, not the extent, of a city that produces demoralization and crime. Wherever a family has a grape-vine, or owns and cultivates a flower-bed, there a voter is sure to be found who cannot be properly enumerated among those who belong to what are termed the "dangerous classes." Mechanics who live in their own houses are safe citizens, and the more of that class that are embraced within the municipal limits of Boston the better will be its government. Crime hides in dark alleys and lanes, and lurks in the shadows of narrow and crooked ways. By studying the plans adopted for the construction of a great city, one can justly measure the degree of effort made by the municipal power controlling it in promoting the character and morality of its people. The influence of openness, of sunlight and pure air, of taste and refinement in laying out a city, ennobles and elevates the character of its inhabitants. The sensitive mind of youth takes its

inclinations and permanent impressions from that
which is most familiar to its eyes and ears, and
the propensity to good or evil of entire communities may thus be formed by the nature of
their surroundings. Man's enjoyment of rural
beauty and natural scenery increases with the
advance of civilization. His higher senses are
satisfied by elements that not only secure to him
health and vigor, but which, at the same time,
gratify his natural desire for recreative amuse-
ments. It is, therefore, by such elements that
he may be lured from those attractions that lead
to pauperism, vice, and crime.* The quality of
the governments of London, Paris and Philadelphia were greatly improved by the extensive enlargement of their territorial area ; and their aston-
ishing progress in wealth and population dates from
the inauguration of liberal and comprehensive views
in planning for their future growth and beauty.
We do not hear of corruption in the administration
of the municipal affairs of the cities of London,

---

* Mr. Olmstead, in speaking of Central Park, New York, says :—

" Every Sunday, in summer, from thirty to forty thousand persons, on
an average, enter the park on foot,—the number on a very fine day being
sometimes nearly a hundred thousand. While most of the grog-shops of
the city were effectually closed by the police under the Excise Law, on
Sunday, the number of visitors to the park was considerably larger than
before. There was no similar increase at the churches.

" Shortly after the park first became attractive, and before any serious
attempt was made to interfere with the Sunday liquor-trade, the head
keeper told me that he saw among the visitors the proprietor of one of
the largest 'saloons' in the city. He accosted him, and expressed some
surprise. The man replied, ' I came to see what the devil you'd got here
that took off so many of my Sunday customers.' "

Paris and Berlin,—one with a population *sixteen times*, another eight times, and the other four times as large as Boston. Can it be said that a government equally as pure cannot be maintained under our Republican system, where education and intelligence attain a higher standard?

Another objection that is seriously urged against the enlargement of Boston as proposed is, that the city will possess power and wealth greater than all the rest of the state.

Sir, that is an objection which I hope does not originate with legislators here. It might possibly be excused in an envious wrangle between city and country boys in a contest at a game of brag, but such a thought should have no place under the dome of this capitol, where questions affecting the best interests of the people of every portion of the Commonwealth are to be intelligently passed upon by their representatives. Upon what basis is it presumed that the people of these different localities are to be less friendly to general state interests because they would be permitted to enjoy greater prosperity under municipal regulations that will best promote their welfare? In what way will the increased wealth and representative power of Boston act prejudicially to the interests of Berkshire, Barnstable, or Essex? If under the sanction of your legislation, the enterprise and growth of Boston shall draw to the waters of her harbor ten ships where one now enters it, will not the towns, har-

bors, and pilots of the Capes be correspondingly
benefited? And if ten trains, where there now is
but one, should climb the mountains of Berkshire
loaded with the productions of the West and de-
scend into the valley of the Connecticut, drawn
thither by the wealth and commercial demands of
Boston, will not Berkshire and Hampden be correspondingly benefited by such increase of trade and
traffic?

Sir, there is not a town or village in the Commonwealth that has not been benefited by the capital and enterprise of Boston; and the suggestion
that an increase of her power and wealth would be
dangerous to the country towns, is ill-timed, unfortunate and ungenerous. Has not her capital been
freely used to build railroads, tunnel mountains and
increase the internal resources of the entire state,
thus increasing the wealth and power of every town
within its limits? If the wealth, population and
power of Boston could, by process of legislation, be
increased tenfold, is it not true that the state at
large would be proportionately benefited? The relations of the state to her metropolis are repre-
sented by the relations of the head to the body.
They are one and inseparable. And I envy not
the heart and sentiments of the citizen who would
knowingly lend himself to the creation of jealousies
between them.

Not wishing further to trench upon your
patience, I must omit the discussion of the most

important subject of sewerage and drainage, as
well as some questions affecting a system of government for the metropolis which for future purposes, whether enlarged as proposed or not, would
need, I presume, some important modifications.
Once more, for a moment, before concluding, I
return to history for an example, and find Boston
situated, with reference to its surroundings, very
much like the city of London, which has been
obliged to absorb more than thirty townships and
boroughs in its suburbs, many of which have now
become as densely populated as the old city upon
which they have crowded so close as to obliterate
all division lines. Fifty-one square miles of the
city are in the county of Middlesex, thirty-six in
Surrey, and thirty-five in Kent, making one hundred twenty-two square miles, and occupying a
part of three counties, as Boston eventually will.

Since 1865 the Parliament of England, ever
zealous, as you know, in guarding the independ-
ence and local rights of boroughs and townships,
have, in connection with the rulers of London, been
engaged in framing an improved system of government for the great metropolis, whose population it
is estimated will reach eight or ten millions, before
the close of the present century. And there is
not a statesman in all England, among the many
who have given an opinion, or who have testified
before a commission similar to the one suggested
in the Resolve under consideration, who does not

assent to the conclusion, that, in order to establish an efficient and economical local government, there must be one central municipal power, with jurisdiction over all the districts at present divided. And to accomplish this end an act has been substantially agreed upon entitled the "Metropolis Municipalities Bill," or "London Corporation Bill." The old independent, disjointed system has become so cumbersome and expensive as to be a serious and alarming burden to the rate-payers of the districts. Such, too, is the experience of the people in and around Boston.

Sir, whoever carefully examines the reports of the financial officers of Boston, and of each of the cities and towns named in the Resolve before us, will be surprised at the magnitude of their public debt—which is being rapidly increased—as well as the sums annually expended by them for public purposes. Much of this money, I hesitate not to declare, would be better thrown into the sea, because, in the absence of any general system applying to all, it is expended in such a way as surely to increase the burdens of taxation hereafter, for the reason that what is now being constructed will have to be demolished to make room for growing necessities not now being provided for.*

* Under the present system of separate governments in the fifteen cities and towns proposed for union with Boston, nearly fifteen hundred persons are required to fill their various local offices; and between four and five thousand octavo pages are used to print the account of their

In Boston, and the cities and towns proposed
for union, there is a population of less than half a
million, and yet it costs more to carry on their
heterogeneous governments than it does that of the
most beautiful, and, with reference to public improvements, the most progressive and best governed city in the world, which contains a population of more than two millions,—showing the cost
of our local governments, *per capita*, to be more
than four times that of the magnificent city of
Paris.

The total debt of Boston and the fifteen cities and
towns named in the Resolve, as exhibited in the following table, was, in 1867, $16,987,233.20.   Their
total debt, 1872, was $37,175,960.69; showing an
increase in a period of five years, since the war—
when their debt should have been on the decrease—
of $20,194,677.49.

doings in their annual reports. If united under one government, in
place of this army of officials, the municipal force would not be increased
by more than two hundred and fifty men, who would perform the services
much better; and certainly, not more than one hundred pages would be
added to the annual reports of the city.

Table showing the increase in the Debt of the following Cities and Towns in a period of Five Years—from 1867 to 1872.

CITIES AND TOWNS.	Debt in 1867.	Rate of taxation on $1,000, 1867.	Debt in 1872.	Rate of taxation on $1,000, 1872.	Increase in five years.
Boston, . .	$12,998,559 91	$12 50	$28,628,535 82	$11 70	$15,629,975 91
Charlestown, .	1,476,073 37	16 50	2,487,547 05	15 40	1,011,473 68
Cambridge, .	1,161,900 22	15 20	2,184,584 42	12 00	1,022,684 20
Chelsea, . .	634,000 00	20 00	1,027,900 00	16 00	393,800 00
Somerville, .	189,474 00	–	593,349 00*	14 00	403,875 00
W. Roxbury, .	No debt.	17 40	288,000 00	10 30	288,000 00
Brookline, .	77,655 96	10 00	575,000 00	8 70	487,344 04
Brighton, .	87,000 00	–	330,002 15	11 00	243,002 15
Watertown, .	51,400 00	–	66,193 00	12 50	14,793 00
Belmont,. .	21,200 00	16 00	18,250 00	12 00	Decrease.
Arlington, .	68,188 71	15 50	216,751 15†	13 50	148,562 41
Medford, .	41,700 00	19 50	270,800 00†	13 80	229,100 00
Malden, .	140,081 00	18 60	367,696 96†	16 80	227,615 96
Everett, . .	Set off in 1870.	–	41,451 11†	12 00	41,451 11
Revere, . .	21,000 00	12 00	44,000 00	13 80	23,000 00
Winthrop, .	16,000 00	19 00	36,000 00	11 50	20,000 00
	$16,987,233 20	–	$37,175,960 69	–	$20,191,677 49

* To 1871 only.   † A part of this sum is for water supply.

What is there to show for this vast expenditure, which has more than doubled this great debt in so brief a period? Have there been any public improvements other than those which should have kept pace with the increase of population, and therefore paid for as they went, from ordinary revenues? If so where are they? Does a continuance of the present system promise economy and progress in those important public works in which we are so lamentably deficient?

Sir, while the Commonwealth is wisely spending millions upon millions to tunnel mountains and create new avenues for feeding the business and commerce of her metropolis, and placing it nearer to the productive regions of the continent, not one step has she taken toward making appropriate provision, even for the natural expansion of her metropolis, to say nothing of that more rapid growth which should be pioneered by noble conception, progressive legislation, and public enterprise.

In the revolutionary period Boston was first in importance in the new-born republic; and, in my judgment she might, under the judicious exercise of state and municipal power, have maintained her supremacy in wealth and population, to the present time. But for lack of administrative foresight in creating home attractions, and in encouraging home enterprises, her young men, and business men, and her capital, have been forced to seek other fields, to build up other cities, and develop the wealth of other states.

What is the matter? Have the people been so intent upon the accumulation of wealth by pursuing the usages of the past, that they have failed to discover the progressive character of the age, or to remember that the sea upon which they are smoothly sailing into the unmeasured future may contain reefs and shoals which cannot be safely passed without soundings, observations, and calculations?

Sir, we have delved in by-gones long enough to be familiar with their lessons, and that is all that we should care to know about them. The past is finished,—the untouched future only is before us. Is it not time that we had paused to take bearings, and learn in which direction the true path of progress lies? Looking down upon the present we find scattered over the territory described in the Resolve before the Senate, Boston broken into municipal fragments,—and while there is but one common interest affecting all, independent governments are maintained in each which are in conflict one with the other. Under such an incongruous system there can be no harmony or method, while both are so essential to public prosperity. I wish here to appeal to your unbiased judgments to substantiate this declaration—that becoming progress in public improvements, economy in official administration, sound sanitary conditions, and contentment among the people, are utterly impossible unless, for general purposes, one homogeneous system of government shall embrace them all. Under the guidance of such a government the ambition of the people, stirred by fresh incentives, would move forward to the achievement of new glories in the fields of progress and civilization. Her business men and capital would come back again, and her young men would be content to build upon foundations illuminated by the brighter destinies of their native metropolis. Thus under the influence of ideas which should lead the progress

11

of Republican civilization, Boston may yet become
the first city on the American continent,—the
favorite resort of those in search of education,
science, thrift in business pursuits, and all that is
healthful, beautiful and grand in nature and art.

APPENDIX.

Professor Holton, who has devoted much attention to civic improvements, and particularly to modes of rapid transit and the transmission of power through tubes, writes me as follows:—

"In your speech I think you have hardly made enough of improvements in the near future. Let us take first the transmission of power. Steam is a perfect vehicle for it. Nothing is needed but a boiler and fire at one end of a tube and an engine at the other. You can turn a faucet and instantly start your machinery. But there is an enormous waste. Every wave of heat that escapes through the walls of the tube is a loss of power; and as soon as the temperature of the interior of the tube falls to 212° no power is left. Every time your engine stops it cools; and power is expended in reheating it to a temperature much over 212° before it will work to its full capacity. The waste is proportioned to the distance between boiler and engine, and every moment's delay is a loss.

"The true method for the transmission of power is by COMPRESSED AIR. Immense steam-engines, miles away and miles apart, convert the power stored in coal into compressed air. They may be aided by the moon (tide-mills), and by the sun (wind-mills), and the owners of them can sell to the city the power which they generate. No street that should have air ' laid on ' could fail of being thronged with manufactures—often such as need but a tenth of a horse-power, or need power but a tenth of the time—unless the merchant should overbid the artisan. For elevators it has this advantage, that lowering reverses the course of the air, and actually throws power back into the tube. Even where not needed for days together, it can be had in large quantities and at a moment's warning. It might be let on to fire-engines the instant that they had reached the fire. It could open a drawbridge, thrust a vessel through, shut it again, and lapse into repose and costlessness. Its pure breath, instead of tainting the workshop, refreshes it. It is transmitted without loss, and can be stored in reservoirs like gas and water.

"But by far the most important use of compressed air would be on local railways, subterranean or elevated. An extravagant head of power would be let on at leaving a station, and a car would near the next at a rate of sixty miles an hour; then the speed would be arrested and stopped simply by reversing the engine and condensing air back into the tank. The waste and wear of braking up is what necessitates low speed on way trains. We could hope to make thirty miles an hour, stops excluded, or a mile in four minutes, including stops. The passengers would go from an eighth of a mile to half the diameter of the city at a uniform rate of three cents, or even less. The great parks would be at the termini of these radiating roads, and the outermost parts of the area they should reach would be as valuable for residences as Commonwealth Avenue is to-day. But the outlay of altering a street, already built, and far too narrow, to suit elevated railways, is something enormous. As to the choice between elevated or underground railroads, I do not hesitate an instant. The average thickness of a city, from cellar-floor to roof, is some eighty feet. The traffic of the streets is only ten feet above its lower plane, and a subterranean road necessitates climbing the moment you leave it. The value of each story diminishes as you rise above the sidewalk. Now if you will put a second sidewalk fifteen feet above the first, and remove to that all the car travel, most of the pedestrians would seek the same level. Ladies who went shopping would not, if they could reach the cars without descending to the ground, go near it once in all their trip. We should have a retail city over the wholesale city. The second story would be more valuable than the first, and an additional value would be given to each floor above.

"The 'Rows' of Chester, England, illustrate the requisite style of building, and we have a single example of it in the Congregational House, corner of Beacon and Somerset streets, Boston. The near approach of the lower story to the centre of the street *does not diminish the light* of the windows opposite. The wall of the first story (invariably of glass and iron) would support the centre of the track. The loading and unloading of carts would little incommode the busy throng of passers, which always increases with the growth of the city. The present size of London would be almost impossible with all the passing on one level.

"Density at the centre is what limits the growth of a city, as it does of a palm. When no more new and tender fibres can penetrate the impacted, hide-bound interior of the palm, growth is arrested. When the centre of a city becomes an inextricable vortex, as now in New York, business seeks to escape from the annoyance to more convenient seats. The question of the ultimate size of a city is then entirely a question of transit.

"On this problem New York is now laboring, but its mechanical exigencies are as nothing compared with the legal obstructions of rivals. London, more fortunate, has made both the upper and lower schemes a success to the passenger; though it is asserted that while the subterranean roads earn no dividends, the elevated ones are doing a good business. The introduction of the best system into Boston, will be like the touch of Ithuriel's spear. London, on the edge of an island and on the banks of a small river, has not the natural advantages of Boston, with its grand harbor and a continent to contribute to it. A century of wise government, with the application to city-transit of the latest improvements in the conveyance of persons, goods and messages, cannot fail to place our metropolis far beyond anything that earth has yet seen."